Dani Binns
Brilliant Builder

Written by Lisa Rajan

Illustrated by Alessia Trunfio

Collins

Chapter 1

Dani Binns found the old toy box in the spare bedroom. Her big sister Tara had suggested choosing a toy from it. Every time Dani picked one, it sent her off to try out a job … and have an exciting adventure.

What toy shall I choose? she thought, looking inside.

Hmm … a ruler?

As she held the ruler, her hand tingled … then her arm … then her whole body.

What job would I need a ruler for? she wondered, as she felt herself spinning away through space and time …

Chapter 2

When Dani opened her eyes, she was on a building site. One of the builders was laying bricks to make a wall.

"Look out!" came a shout behind her.

Dani jumped. The ruler flew out of her hand and over the wall. She spun around.

"Sorry!" called a boy pouring sloppy wet concrete right where she was standing.

Dani scrambled out of the way.

"Sorry!" the boy exclaimed again. "I'm Tai.
Grab a hard hat, gloves and high-vis vest.
Could you please help Asha build that wall?"

He pointed at a girl waving a trowel.
She showed Dani how to lay a row of bricks.

Dani tried it herself. It was harder
than it looked.

"Oh dear," Dani sighed as she scanned her
wonky line of bricks.

"My ruler will help to make it straight!"
she said, looking for it over the wall.

"You'll have to go through the house to get it,"
replied Asha. "Can you fetch the wheelbarrow
too, please?"

Chapter 3

Dani stumbled through the half-built house and down the front steps. She found the ruler and put it in the wheelbarrow.

On her way back, she saw a family looking at the finished house next door. They looked sad.

Dani reached the steps. How was she going to get a wheelbarrow up them?

She pulled the wheelbarrow up backwards. *Bump ... bump ... bump!*

The ruler bounced out.

Dani finally reached the top step. She bobbed down to pick up the ruler and put it back in the wheelbarrow.

But now she had a new problem.
The wheelbarrow wouldn't fit through
the doorway!

The doorway wasn't wide enough.

She tipped the wheelbarrow on to its side and managed to wobble it through. *Oops!* The ruler bounced out again. This was tricky.

"Phew," Dani puffed when she finally made it back to Asha.

"Who's going to live in this house when it's finished?" asked Dani, as Tai put the wheelbarrow by the cement mixer.

"Anyone, I suppose …" replied Asha, "… a family, probably."

"Not the family I saw," said Dani. "It was hard enough to get a wheelbarrow up the steps and through the door, let alone a wheelchair. No wonder that family looked sad."

13

Chapter 4

"People can adapt the house later if they need to," said Tai. "They can swap the steps for a ramp and widen the doorways."

"True," said Dani, "but if we made those changes now, the house would be easy to live in for *anyone* and *everyone*. People with pushchairs, people who find steps difficult – everyone!"

"What a brilliant idea!" cheered Asha and Tai.

Tai showed Dani the building plans.
Dani suggested lots of changes that made
the house easier to enter and move around.

"How much wider should the doorways be?"
Asha asked Dani.

"I'll measure the wheelchair," smiled Dani.
"Now, where's my ruler?"

It was in the wheelbarrow, which was under the cement mixer … and about to catch a big sloppy dollop of concrete!

Asha darted forward and grabbed the ruler, just in time.

"Thank you!" said Dani. "We'll need it to measure the wheelchair and the doorways. And then you can keep it for the next house you build."

"It was your brilliant, caring and practical idea that made the house fit for everyone," said Tai, "not the ruler. *You* take it as a souvenir of your adventure."

As Asha handed Dani the ruler, Dani felt her hand tingle. Then her arm tingled. Then her whole body started spinning and tumbling away from the building site …

Chapter 5

When the spinning stopped, Dani found herself back in the spare bedroom. She put the ruler in the toy box and closed the lid.

"What a fantastic adventure!" she told her sister Tara. "The ruler helped me to design and build a brand new house. I think I'll be a builder when I grow up!"

Tara smiled. "The toy box helps build big dreams, Dani," she said. "I wonder if future adventures will measure up?"

Dani's practical idea

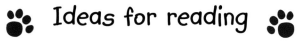 Ideas for reading

Written by Clare Dowdall, PhD
Lecturer and Primary Literacy Consultant

Reading objectives:
- discuss the sequence of events in books and how items of information are related
- discuss and clarify the meanings of words, linking new meanings to known vocabulary
- make inferences on the basis of what is being said and done
- predict what might happen on the basis of what has been read so far

Spoken language objectives:
- use relevant strategies to build their vocabulary
- gain, maintain and monitor the interest of the listener(s)

Curriculum links: Design technology: Designing and making; Mathematics: Measurement

Interest words: concrete, cement, high-vis, trowel, wheelbarrow, adapt, practical, souvenir

Resources: rulers and tape measures, whiteboard and pens, paper and pencils

Build a context for reading

- Look at the front cover and talk about what Dani is doing. Ask children for their experiences of building work – in their home, school or local community.
- Read the blurb together. Check that children can read the word *concrete* and *measure*. Introduce the other interest words on a whiteboard to aid independent reading.
- List any other equipment that children know is involved in building to develop children's vocabulary further.
- Ask children to predict what Dani might learn to do in this story.

Understand and apply reading strategies

- Ask for a volunteer to begin reading aloud on pp2–3. Model using appropriate expression and the punctuation to add effect.